1906:
Every Man For Himself!

1906:
Every Man For Himself!

edited by
Maisie Robson, M.A.

Eynsford Hill Press
2002

© Maisie Robson, 2002

Typeset and Published by
Eynsford Hill Press
14 New Street
Wombwell
Barnsley
South Yorkshire
S73 0AE

ISBN 0 9542318 0 5

All rights reserved. No part of this publication may be copied, reproduced or stored without the consent of the publisher.

British Library Cataloguing in Publication Data
A catalogue record for this book is available from the British Library.

Printed and bound in Great Britain
by Prontaprint, Barnsley, South Yorkshire

CONTENTS

	Page
Editor's Introduction	6
Part One: Every Man for Himself!	7
Shopkeeping in a Nutshell	7
Shopkeeping for Men: Concluding Observations	28
Our Millions of Producing Operatives	31
Postscript: Emigration to the Colonies	39
Part Two: What Shall we do with Our Girls?	40
The Lady Shopkeeper	40
Principal Careers for Women	45
Part Three: Upstairs, Downstairs	54
Duties of Domestic Servants, Great and Small	54

EDITOR'S INTRODUCTION

To anyone born after the War, the England of 1906 is a foreign land: a quarter of the globe was pink, and to be called an "Imperialist" was a compliment, not a curse. Florence Nightingale had four more years to live, Charlie Chaplin was a mere teenager and a pound sterling could be exchanged for 4.86 American dollars. Certain trades were beginning to feel disquiet about the effect of the motor car on their business (women were buying fewer hats!), but life had not changed all that much since Waterloo. So was this the bland and gentle pre-1914 world described nostalgically by Philip Larkin in his poem "MCMXIV" — "Never such innocence again"?

While researching a book on Arthur Mee, I came across a curious part-work Mee edited between 1906 and 1907, splendidly entitled *The Harmsworth Self-Educator*. This fortnightly magazine, 136 pages per issue, covered every topic under the sun — from teach yourself Latin, to the origins of the universe, to more practical matters such as how to start a shop on £50 capital, and whether ladies should work outside the home. The slippery yellow pages tell an extraordinary story of everyday heroism: the story of our grandparents' and great-grandparents' struggle for dignity and survival.

The lower middle-class and the "respectable" working class of Edwardian England had an unquenchable desire to improve their lot in life, and an indifferent education at a Board School, ending at age 14, left them insecure and hungry for knowledge. This was the vast potential readership for the *Self-Educator*, and its editor Arthur Mee, brought up in poverty in Nottingham and sent out to work at 14, knew his reader intimately.

The present editor has mined the 7000+ pages (each page two columns of 8-point type) for contemporary material which illuminates living conditions at the turn of the last century. The work, wages and hours described in Parts One and Two speak for themselves, but the *mutual* degradation revealed in Part Three, on domestic service, is equally chilling.

Despite Mr Larkin's lovely poem, the pages of the *Self-Educator*, reproduced here in the contributors' own words, lead me to conclude there was nothing "innocent" or gentle about England before 1914 — rather, it was

Every Man For Himself!

PART ONE: EVERY MAN FOR HIMSELF!

Shopkeeping in a Nutshell

☞ The following list details briefly the conditions usually prevailing in the chief shopkeeping trades. It has been carefully compiled from authoritative sources.

☞ From most shopkeeping trades the system of indenturing apprentices has almost disappeared.

☞ The sum recommended as capital is the minimum upon which a start can be made with any prospect of success.

☞ It is certain that if you follow these precepts and are prepared and determined to work hard and give all your time to the care of your business, it will not be many years before you are the proprietor of a business employing many hands besides your own.

Baby-Carriage dealers
The vendor of baby-carriages seldom confines himself to their sale. Occasionally they may constitute the backbone of a business, but more often they are merely a branch of a more important trade, such as that of the ironmonger, the house furnisher, the cycle or sewing machine agent, or the draper. As the trade, under British climatic conditions, is strictly a seasonal one, the vendor of baby-carriages pure and simple finds nothing to occupy him during the winter months, so that his profits and turnover during the selling season must be fairly large to permit successful trading upon such a basis. There are some classes of shops with which the sale of baby-carriages goes well — as, for instance, that of a domestic laundry machine depôt, which has its busiest period during the winter months. The summer trade in baby-carriages equalises business somewhat. On the other hand, it is an awkward adjunct to the business of a cycle agent, as both departments are under pressure during the same months of the year.

The stock takes up a good deal of room, hence the trade can be conducted properly only by the shopkeeper who possesses the necessary accommodation. A shop with an open window is the best for the dealer. It permits street passengers to see the assortment, and the parents — especially if baby be the firstborn — are most particular in their choice.

Fashion must be studied, especially by the man new to the business. Above all, expensive carriages should be ordered sparingly. The cheap article is that in which the bulk of the trade is done. The last few years have witnessed a wave of popularity for the light, collapsible baby-vehicle, termed the go-cart or push-cart. This is not good for the infant occupant, and bad for the trade. This type of vehicle is in diminished favour, but it will always have a certain acceptance by the flat dweller, who finds every square inch of house-room a matter of consideration, and by the parent who migrates to the seaside. The latter may transport it thither, and thereby save the expense of hiring a baby-carriage during the holiday.

The dealer who makes baby-carriages a prominent department should strain every effort to be looked upon in his neighbourhood as the leading man for such goods. The trade is particularly susceptible to influence by advertisement in the local newspapers. We have known excellent results attained by the practice of posting a neat price list and circular to the addresses given in the birth columns of the local press.

The repairing of baby-carriages is not an extensive trade, but it is exceedingly remunerative. The stock necessary for its prosecution is not large — an assortment of indiarubber tyres, a few brass axle-caps, and some handles being almost all that is necessary. Tyre-fitting pays well. The rubber tyre may cost not more than 10d. per pound, and a charge of 5s. or 6s. for fitting four wheels with new tyres will show a profit of half the price, even allowing for the labour of fixing.

Baker and confectioner
Regular apprenticeships not general. Lads are engaged at about 6s. a week; journeymen bakers earn from 25s. to 35s., foremen rising higher. Capital required to start a bakery equipped with machinery, £150 and upwards.

Barbers
In ordinary barbering and hairdressing, apprenticeship varies in length from

two to seven years. Boys receive about 2s.6d. per week to begin; assistants earn from 21s. to 32s. plus commissions on articles sold. Businesses may easily be started on £50 capital. For a steady and aspiring journeyman barber, there is good opportunity for a start in business. The amount of capital required will necessarily depend on the class of establishment to be opened. A modest barber's shop, pure and simple, may be attempted with about £25, and in this case the usual charges for attendance are 1½d. for shaving and 3d. for haircutting. Only rude saloon fittings would be requisite, and practically no stock, the trade being small. After paying a lather boy or apprentice, rent, and other attendant expenses, a plain barber would expect to derive a net income for himself of £2 to £2.10s. per week. The work is hard and the hours long. Cheap labour is employed, young men often being taken who wish to pick up the rudiments of the trade without serving an apprenticeship.

The question of saloon sanitation has occupied the attention of the public, of the trade, and of municipal authorities during the past two years or more. The question of scientific sanitation of saloons was brought to a climax in London in 1903 by the production of a code of regulations and recommendations. What the financial bearing of this agitation may ultimately be upon the fittings and upkeep of barbers' saloons and upon the charges for services which they may find it necessary to levy cannot now be stated, seeing that for the present barbers may voluntarily register under this code, or may reject it, or adopt any portion of it as they personally desire.

Booksellers
Conditions similar to those for stationers, but double capital required. There are some trades which, though by no means extremely profitable to those who engage in them, have at least the advantage of being pleasant to pursue, and of these we may say that none is pleasanter than bookselling.

We have met booksellers who had better have taken to butchering or innkeeping, so ignorant and indifferent were they to the interesting features of their work, having, for instance, never heard of some well-known authors. These are round pegs in square holes and we must not stay to consider them, but need only urge that no man who is not naturally fond of handling — not necessarily reading — books, and who is not interested in the names of authors and the works they have written, should contemplate for one moment the business of bookselling with any hope of succeeding therein.

As every successful man begins in some humble position in the trade in which he has made up his mind to excel, we begin with the bookseller's assistant. Given the taste for books, a good memory, and a bright address, hardly anyone who desires to become a bookseller need fail of the opportunity. There is no formal apprenticeship nowadays, and the conditions of employment will vary in every town, if not with every employer. In London, a youth will be taken on at 10s. or 12s. a week to learn the business, and in the course of five or six years— but largely according to the ability he displays — he will be accounted a fully-qualified assistant, his salary varying from 30s. to £2 a week. A chief assistant, where the proprietor is manager, will seldom get more than £3 a week, and £4 would be thought a good wage for one in charge of a considerable bookselling business. In the provinces a lower scale of wages is the rule; but as living expenses are much less than in London, the remuneration is proportionately as good.

While we deprecate the presumptuous assistant urging his views on literature upon customers who, in all likelihood, are much better informed than himself, we must point out the need to be alert in placing new books before every likely buyer, cultivating the habit of pleasing conversation, and freely showing any work of unusual interest to the customer who seems interested in inspecting the stock.

Boots and shoes
Practical apprenticeship five years and wages 5s. to 14s.; journeymen earn from 25s. to 35s. Girls usually engaged as messenger girls at 2s.6d. per week. Capital required to start, £120. Shop assistance in the boot-selling trade is not highly paid. In the cities a lad may be had at from 10s. to 15s. a week, and in the provinces girls are often employed at from 2s.6d. to 10s. a week. Even in London a good, smart, all-round assistant can be had for 8s. a week, so that assistants' salaries do not account for an undue proportion of the dead charges in the boot retailing business.

The terms upon which boots are sold depend upon the locality and the nature of the trade. In the cities it is nearly all of a cash description, but in the family trade in the provinces the credit turnover may rise to 50 per cent of the total. An iniquitous practice has crept into the trade. It is by no means general, but sufficiently common for notice and stricture here. It is not unusual that an assistant may reap benefit by "fleecing the greenhorns". If it be evident that a customer is ignorant of boots and not particular as to price, the assistant may sell a 10s.6d. boot for, say, 12s.6d. or 14s.6d., and thereby pocket a considerable commission, say, half the excess. On moral grounds the practice is to be condemned, but even on the lower grounds of business policy it is questionable if it can be really remunerative.

Butchers

Errand boy engaged at about 5s. weekly and left to work his way up. An assistant salesman going the rounds with pony and trap receives 30s. to 40s.; shop salesman usually a little less. Cash business may be started on £50; credit business on £150 to £200.

Chemists and druggists

Premiums of £20 to £100 required in apprenticing to high-class chemists in England. Such apprentices live indoors. Ordinary unindentured outdoors. Apprenticeship wages, 4s., 5s., 6s., 7s., weekly; four years' apprenticeship the rule in both cases. Assistants' wages 20s. to 30s. per week for unqualified men, and 30s. to 50s. for qualified assistants. The best positions are as dispensers in public institutions, or as employees of the large drug stores. Capital required to start a pharmacy, £300.

Not more than two per cent of chemists live by pharmacy alone. The adjuncts to the chemist's trade provide livelihoods for the other 98 per cent. Twenty years ago these adjuncts, such as proprietaries (or patent medicines as they are more often called), perfumes, toilet articles, and fancy goods bore a fair profit. But within recent years departmental stores have opened drug sections where proprietaries, perfumes, and the more popular household preparations commonly obtained from the chemist, are sold as a draw at almost cost prices. This principle of cutting prices has extended enormously within the past few years, much to the detriment of the chemist's calling. Many qualified chemists themselves started the "cutting" scheme, and limited companies calling themselves "cash chemists" have sprung into being and make a virtue of low prices. This parlous state of things has been mitigated somewhat, however, by the work done by the Proprietary Articles Trade Association.

Commercial travellers

The highways of commercial travelling are strewn with the wrecks of men of ambition, ability, and promise who have succumbed to the temptations of the road. The rock upon which most careers have split has been that of drink. The virtue of hospitality is frequently exercised by the commercial traveller in the ordinary course of his business, and too often it has led to excessive tippling. This is not the place to preach total abstinence, but if any class of men have reason to protect themselves against the dangers of alcohol, it is that of commercial travellers. The young commercial who begins by the determination to refuse to do business which depends upon "treating" fortifies himself against the danger that has betrayed thousands of his fellows. Fortunately the practice of "standing treat" is not nearly so general as it used to be.

We cannot leave the subject of commercial travellers without mentioning the greater saving of time which many of them will be able to effect by the use of motor-cars. For city work the motor shows to little advantage. For men who take with them a wide range of samples, it is undoubtedly good, as one call may be made after another with greater speed, and more work may therefore be done in a day by its use. Also the chauffeur is more available for assisting the traveller with samples and cases, because the motor-car may stand by the kerb without the attention required when a horse is between the shafts.

But the most important sphere for the commercial traveller's motor-car is in country districts with infrequent train service. We are convinced that the commercial community do not yet realise what the motor-car may mean for them in this respect, and believe that there is a rich harvest for firms who adopt it as a conveyance for commercial travellers.

Shopkeepers in villages are often denied the privilege of buying from samples, and instead of the numerous sample-cases opened out before town buyers, a small hand-bag and a bulky catalogue serves for the village shopkeeper. The motor may be made a travelling sample-room, and the journey will cost less than it formerly did without samples.

Cutlery and tool dealers

The retailer of tools and cutlery must have an intimate knowledge of the wares he offers. No class of customers is more difficult to please than that of artisans who have occasion to purchase implements of their handicrafts. Details which seem to the unsophisticated spectator unimportant to the point of triviality are, to the workman, vital to good work and essential to his acceptance.

This consideration is the main reason for the possibility of successful trading by the small man of the proper type in face of all the competition which capital and organisation can pit against him. The dealer who will listen to all the objections of the exacting purchaser, who will appreciate his point of view if he cannot accept all his criticisms as reasonable, and who can exhibit a practical acquaintance with the use of tools, is always preferred by the artisan tool buyer to the ironmonger's assistant whose knowledge of tools is not deeper than that gained by unpacking and pricing them.

Thus the smart workman with business capacity who ventures into the field of shopkeeping as a dealer in workman's tools need seldom fear the issue provided he select a district where workmen frequent the shopping thoroughfares, and if there are not too many of his own kind already exploiting the same trade.

Drapers

Apprenticeships usually three to four years and wages 6s., 7s., 8s., 9s., per week; assistants make 16s. to 30s. Living-in apprentices receive no wages, but may receive small commissions on sales during the latter half of term. Living-in assistants receive £20 to £30 a year. Female apprentices not common; female assistants receive 8s. to 20s. a week, or if living in up to £15 per year. Capital required for small drapery business, £200. Capital should be turned over four times a year.

In ages that are past the draper was a man who sold cloth; today he is a merchant who deals in a heterogeneous assortment of goods, with drapery as an unobtrusive side line. For drapery, properly so called, means cloth and stuff goods, household and personal linen, white cotton piece-goods (or "longcloths"), cottons and calicoes, Irish linen, tablecloths, serviettes, blankets, towelling, prints, flannel, etc. All these things, of course, are necessaries of the trade of a draper still, but the present day retailer finds that there are many other lucrative adjuncts to his business — more profitable and easier to handle and to stock — that the present generation of purchasers demands. Indeed, so general has become the business that there seem scarcely any goods of the "fancy" character which the modern draper of any pretensions does not find it profitable to handle.

As a rule, it is better to start off one's own bat than to buy a going concern. This rule applies more particularly to businesses in a big town for town people appear rather to prefer going to a new shop. The blasé inhabitants of large cities are ever on the look-out for new sensations, and a new adventure attracts them, more often than not, on account of its novelty.

In an old-established country establishment nearly half the business done is credit, and therefore a longer profit is necessary. It is a common thing to find in such businesses that the majority of the customers are never off the books. The servant girl comes in for a dress, she pays £1 down, and the balance remains. When she has paid off that, she wants something else, and so it goes on.

An elaboration of this system is practised on an enormous scale particularly in the Midlands and Lancashire by tallymen, or "Scotch drapers", as they are usually designated. These descendants of the ancient packman or travelling draper have regular rounds of customers in the districts in which they settle, upon whom they call periodically with samples of dress-stuffs and drapery. A sum is paid down, and the balance is collected in so many shillings weekly, fortnightly, or monthly as the case may be. Naturally, the purchaser has to pay considerably more than the value of the goods, but it is a convenience for poor people, and incidentally, the tallymen usually make small fortunes in a surprisingly short time.

Fishmongers

This is distinctly one of the businesses in which an untrained person is most likely to come to grief. Occasionally, gentlemen's servants, who have acquired, as they imagine, a more or less intimate knowledge of buying in fairly large quantities for their master's table, think they know all that is needed to embark on a retail business. There can be no greater mistake, for buying is only one of the many things necessary; cutting up and selling are totally different, more particularly when the cutting and selling must be done in such a careful manner as to secure a profit sufficient to pay the rent of a shop, the taxes, the help required, the keep of a man — with probably a wife and family to boot — and the saving of a little money for the proverbial rainy day. So the butler who invests his savings in a fishmongery business more often than not invites financial disaster. The best way to learn the trade is from the "basket", so to speak, upwards.

Fruiterers

We will assume here a young man who has a fairly accurate knowledge of buying and selling fresh fruit, is not daunted by fear of costers or aught else, and has determined to start on his own account. First of all he must have saved or acquired a capital of £60 to £100, and competent fruiterers state that, especially for a young man, a wife is an absolute essential. The advantages of a working matrimonial partner, with an equal interest in the success of the young concern, are obvious.

The beginner should see that he has the right to at least a few feet of forecourt in front of his window or beside his door to display some of his goods direct to his customers without the intervention of glass. The fruit-buying public nowadays exhibit a liking for seeing the fruit at close quarters, and a good deal of fruit retailing is done on the pavement in front of the shop.

It is probable that many of the British Colonies in the Southern Hemisphere will attain an increasing importance as sources of both fruits and vegetables for the British market. Efforts are being put forth by many Colonial Governments to ensure that exported fruits shall be carefully selected and packed, so that a reputation for quality may be achieved.

Fur merchants

It is impossible to state definitely what a man must buy, for the changes of fashion in furs are as erratic and unaccountable as the changes in the weather. This year there may be a run on chinchilla, next year on marmot, the season following on marten, and so on. Sables are about the only fur that may be considered permanently fashionable; but there is not only the fur, but the style of garment to be considered. Jackets of Empire style, loose sacs, boleros, and so forth, may each or all be the rage of the season. Last season there was a run on fur toques and fur hats of various shapes for ladies, and the practice of wearing stoles loosely thrown back over the shoulders necessitated a difference in shapes. White hare was in great demand (also dyed to imitate fox). Squirrel also is most fashionable. The man of experience keeps his eyes wide open, then, on that mysterious female entity — whoever she may be — "who sets the fashion".

Furniture dealers
In the practical side, departmentalism has nearly killed the general apprenticeship system. Where apprentices are taken time is usually for five years, beginning at 4s. or 5s. and rising to 8s. or 10s. Journeymen workers earn 7d. to 11d. an hour. Salesmen frequently begin as message boys at 5s. a week and work their way up. Assistant salesmen begin at about 20s. to 25s. a week, and may rise to several hundreds a year in best shops. Trade usually allied to general house furnishing. Modest business may be set up on £100-£200, but present tendency is towards hire-purchase trading, which requires much more capital.

To a young man there are few trades affording such excellent opportunities as that of general furnishing. Of course, some capital is necessary, but brains are more so, and, given plenty of grit, there is no reason why success should not be attained. No better experience can be gained than that of working through the various departments of some of the very large firms, to acquire a general knowledge which will prove eminently useful when the budding shopkeeper starts on his own account. The department which calls for the most careful study is the carpet section, for it is only by constantly handling carpets and rugs that the fingers get so sensitive that clever buyers are able to judge these goods so exactly and closely that the small difference of ½d. per yard in quality is noticeable to them.

It may not be out of place to refer to the hire system here. Infinite care must be taken to be sure of the reliability of the person to be trusted with the goods. Even greater care will have to be taken with all entries in the books, a system of inquiry as to the status of the individual wanting the goods, means by which defaulting customers can be pressed for the instalments, and also a system for tracing "runaways". Although larger figures due to increased profit from this class of trade may look well in your day books, please do not reckon it as all profit until you have collected the cash.

Gentlemen's outfitters
The exterior of the shop should be painted white or stone colour, and a good glass fascia and stall boards should be fitted. If space permits, money should be spent on one or two small outside wall cases, which should always be neatly dressed with the latest novelties marked in plain figures. Such cases, if properly attended to, will be very remunerative. External fittings such as

we have indicated will cost about £15. The window enclosure must be made dust-proof, and ought to be fitted with a large side mirror, so as to give the effect of space. A good variety of window fittings ought to be bought — brass rods with movable brackets, shirt stands, telescopic stands, and a glass shelf, or more than one, along the front of the window. The sum of £15 upon the window interior should not be considered too much.

The expense of shop assistance will not be great at the start. An apprentice engaged for three years may be had for 5s., 7s.6d. and 10s. per week during the respective years, and in provincial towns wages are lower still. When an assistant salesman has to be engaged, he will demand £2 per week in the city, if a good man, with probably commission on his sales. The usual commission is 1¼ per cent, and this will make an addition of 15s. per week, on the average, to the assistant's wages.

Some districts are favourably situated for pushing trade in outfits for hot and cold climates. When the shop of the gentlemen's outfitter is so situated its proprietor should not fail to take advantage of his opportunities. This department should be encouraged by the publication of a printed list showing details of a wide range of goods suitable for foreign countries with climates different from our own. That everything shown in the list is not kept in stock matters little. Special articles can always be got without delay, and the man about to go abroad does not require his outfit at five minutes' notice.

Greengrocers
The sale of vegetables is one of growing importance. To the young man, therefore, with a good constitution and a working knowledge of the business, it offers a fine field for intelligent enterprise. The necessary knowledge is easily acquired by a smart, wide-awake man, and provided he has also been prudent and careful to the extent of saving £50 or £60, he may fairly consider himself equipped for a start on his own account. If, besides the qualifications, he has acquired a partner in life to share his joys and sorrows, and to help him in his business, so much the better.

In these days when competition is so keen, it behoves the beginner to bestir himself and look out for orders. It is of no use to stand in the shop and expect the neighbourhood to flock to your establishment when there are countless peripatetic vendors of vegetables and fruit in the shape of persistent costers, who buy the "left" stocks in the market for next to nothing, and who vend particular articles from door to door in your neighbourhood at probably cheaper prices than you are selling in your rented shop. It will be imperative, therefore, either to go personally, or to send out a boy every morning to solicit orders for the dinner vegetables needed by the residents of the neighbourhood.

Grocers

The apprenticeship system is becoming less usual, but where it exists it is from three to four years. Wages, 6s., 8s., 10s., 12s. Assistants earn from 17s. to 28s. Capital required, £170 to £200. Stock should be turned over eight times a year.

Haberdashers

Haberdashery is suitable for exploitation as a separate trade by, say, a draper who has advanced in life, and finds himself out of employment at an age when he cannot get another. We know several men who have done much better for themselves by such a venture than they could have done by taking another situation even had they been able to find one.

Haberdashery comprises all manner of "small wares" connected with the making of garments — needles, pins, bodkins, cottons, tapes, and such things — which are in everyday demand everywhere. The trade or the department is commonly considered a paltry one, as nearly everything sold is of low price; but it requires, perhaps for that reason, greater attention to detail if it is to be successful. The "bump" of orderliness must be well developed in the haberdasher, else the multitude of small articles of which his stock is composed will become hopelessly confused, and render the prompt service of customers impossible.

Hairdressers

As distinct from ordinary barbers, hairdressers serve no apprenticeship, but may receive instruction in one of the hairdressers' schools in London and the provincial cities. Salaries for artists in ladies' hairdressing are usually from two to three guineas a week, plus commission.

Ironmongers

Apprenticeship usually four years, and wages, 4s., 5s., 6s., 7s. Assistants earn 20s. to 40s. Capital required to start general ironmongery business, £600. Stock should be turned over twice a year.

Jewellers

A premium of £50 to £100 is usually paid when a youth enters as apprentice, the premium being returned in the form of wages during service. Apprenticeship terminates at the age of 21. A journeyman jeweller earns from 27s. to 50s. per week. The best working jewellers in London, the seat of the English trade, are foreigners — French, Belgian, Swiss. Capital required to start business with small stock, £500. Good men have stock on consignment from wholesale houses or manufacturers. In the mixed watch-making and jewelling trade of the provinces a seven years apprenticeship is common, wages beginning at 5s. and rising to 12s.

Licensed victuallers

The trade of the licensed victualler is not usually regarded as a branch of shopkeeping. Although there is no fundamental reason for this, the view is to some extent justified by the great differences that exist between the conditions of selling excisable liquors and those of all other branches of retailing. No other trade is so encompassed and hedged about with laws, so subject to legal regulation in all its details, or so great an object of the attentions of social reformers and zealots.

A good training for a landlord of small capital, new to his responsibilities, is afforded by a tenancy — under brewers of standing, of course — in a semi-working-class neighbourhood, where most of the houses are classed as "small property", and where there are plenty of people walking about. Beer is the article mostly sold, for the English working man drinks little or no spirits. The day trade in the jug department will also be good. Brewers' rents for these houses are very variable, and are usually more than the ordinary rental of the property. They may be anything from £50 to £100.

Keeping the licence when it is obtained is not an easy matter. It may be directly forfeited upon conviction for seven particular offences, including felony, keeping a disorderly house, selling spirits without a spirit licence, and making inter-communication between licensed and unlicensed premises. Further, convictions for serving drunken persons or children under 14 in open vessels, allowing the premises to be used for betting, gambling, or allowing customers to be on the premises, or billiards to be played, after prohibited hours, are entered upon the Register of Licences, and regard is had to them by the justices when a renewal or transfer is wanted. The staff must be very wide awake to prevent betting slips being passed, though it is very difficult to detect this. If the loser of a bet pays it by paying for drinks it is an offence under the Gaming Act.

Newsagents

In the present state of society the newsagent is as essential a part of modern life as the printer and the reporter, and there should be no difficulty in anyone with the ambition of becoming a disseminator of news finding a suitable sphere for his activities.

The amount of capital required to start depends entirely on the ideas of the beginner. For instance, he may select a stand in a busy thoroughfare, or a pitch near a railway station, where a constant stream of men passes morning and evening, and, with the expenditure of a few shillings, obtain and dispose of a supply of the morning and evening papers. Or he may ally himself with one particular newspaper, and obtain from the manager a district, which he is expected to work for all that he is worth. The latter class are familiarly known as "hawkers", and some people are squeamish about venturing on such a course. A good wage, however, is usually made right away, and there are no expenses to come off.

Presuming, however, that the aspirant wishes to blossom forth at once as a shopkeeper, one of two courses is open to him: first, to acquire a business which, for some reason or other, has come into the market; or, secondly, to select a shop, preferably in some busy thoroughfare. With regard to the former course, that of acquiring a business as a going concern, the utmost caution must be exercised by the buyer, as frequently, despite the specious reasons given by the seller, those businesses which come into the market are either suffering from "dry rot", or have got into the sere and yellow leaf.

Anyone going in for the newsvendor business must make up his mind for a life of hard work and strenuous endeavour. It is not the line for the Tired Tims and Weary Willies. To do the work thoroughly he must be up early and work late. He must go to the publishing offices or attend the arrival of the early morning trains himself and see that his army of boys are all forward and supplied with the papers for their various districts; and, in the event of one or more not turning up, he must arrange for others to take their places.

There is no business in which there are more worries and petty annoyances. The newsagent will have much to try his temper, and while avoiding servility on the one hand will find the business of the newsagent an excellent school for cultivating the virtues of patience and courtesy, without which he will invariably fail.

Opticians

One of the few businesses which are not overcrowded, and where a competence is fairly certain to those electing to follow it. Employers prefer technically trained youths instead of apprentices. Instruction in optics is conveyed at Northampton Institute, London. Assistants easily earn 40s. to 60s. a week, and managers rise as high as £500 a year. A sight-testing optician may begin business on £250-£350 capital, but to embrace the trade in all its branches £1000 is necessary.

Pawnbrokers

Apprenticeship practically unknown. Warehouse boys usually live in, and receive, in addition to board and lodging, £6 or £8 a year. Assistants earn 30s. a week; managers in first-class establishments from £250 to £300 a year. Many who enter the trade leave it for other vocations. A merchant business is usually incorporated with pawnbroking proper. Capital necessary, £2000.

Of all the careers open to a man on fortune bent there is perhaps none less inviting than that pursued by the pawnbroker. For ages he has been covered with obloquy, regarded as a pariah by society, and made a scapegoat of by those whose business it is to restore property to unfortunate persons whom thieves have despoiled. The whole trade of pawnbroking has been stigmatised as dishonourable, and the pawnbrokers themselves as little better than criminals.

Whatever has been the truth in the past, pawnbroking is now carried on in the light of day. Its operations are controlled by statute, while its followers are invariably men esteemed by their customers and neighbours. No other tradesman except, perhaps, the licensed victualler, is surrounded by law as the pawnbroker. The Act of Parliament regulating the trade actually bristles with penalties for the infringement of any of its sections, almost any one of which may be put in motion upon application to a magistrate. It speaks well, therefore, for the members of the trade that so few charges of any importance have been brought home to them. Still the bad name has stuck to them as to the proverbial dog.

The pawnbroker has to avoid taking in pledge property not lawfully acquired, or to which the pawner cannot confer a good title. "Duffing" or "mosking" is a career pursued throughout the country with considerable success. It consists of purchasing or manufacturing goods, and pledging them at a profit. Numbers are engaged in it, making their way from shop to shop, and from town to town, until they have succeeded in persuading some unwary pawnbroker to advance them the sum they are prepared to accept.

There is no royal road to pawnbroking. It cannot be learned or conducted by rule of thumb, but demands from its followers sheer hard work and close application; neither can it be imparted through the pages of a book. The pawnbroker must keep his nose to the grindstone all day long, and the man who succeeds in making a competence at the business would probably do so far more quickly in any other industry.

Photographers

Apprenticeship prevails, but not common. Usual length four years, beginning at 3s. or 4s. a week and rising to 10s. Assistant operators earn 20s. to 50s. Business is often attempted with success on a very few pounds, but to equip a studio properly demands £100 to £200.

Picture Postcard Dealers

Like its near relative the Christmas card, the picture postcard originated on the Continent, and from very small beginnings rapidly developed into a flourishing business long ere it took hold of the British public. But today there is not a town or hamlet in the United Kingdom where the picture postcard has not penetrated. The sale of picture postcards is not confined to any trade, but may be undertaken by anyone who has a shop or a window to show them, and no special training is necessary for the sale of them.

The picture postcard has come to stay. It may readily be added as a valuable adjunct to almost any business, especially to that of the fancy stationer, who will find in it more than a compensation for the decrease in the sale of notepaper. For there is no doubt that since the advent of the picture postcard, letter writing has to a large extent gone out of fashion.

Now a word of warning. All dealers should beware of allowing anything vulgar, indecent, or suggestive of indecency, to creep into stock. There have been and there are such cards on the market, and there are dealers vile enough to engage in the traffic. The British public is clean minded, and will on no account tolerate this. Nothing will more quickly kill this business than the publication and sale of such filth. The Stationery Trades Association is aware of this fact, and we are glad to note, has taken up a strong position in regard to it. It rests with dealers themselves to be vigilant in stamping it out, and they will find that they have, as a rule, loyal allies in the magistrates and police throughout the country.

Post Office Sub-Agents

We are here dealing with a sub-office which is under a district office, and is undertaken by a shopkeeper as an addition to his ordinary trade. Such a combination offers distinct advantages to him. It introduces customers who, when once on the premises, take the opportunity of making purchases. Then, the profits reaped from the postal department are by no means to be despised.

Naturally, certain businesses are tabooed by the authorities. In villages the office is frequently located in the shop of a general dealer or draper, but in towns or suburban districts those most favoured are chemists, stationers, confectioners and grocers, and sometimes, though rarely, bakers. A post-office, for obvious reasons, is seldom granted to a man holding a licence for the sale of wines and spirits. Occasionally the grant is withdrawn; it would be so were gambling or betting known to take place in the shop.

A postmaster in a village may get the small salary of £10 or £12. A certain busy grocer in a suburban district is allowed the somewhat nominal "responsibility" salary of £48, increased later to £50; but he gets a good commission on certain sales — out of which, however, he has to pay his staff. The postmaster has no information as to the working out of commissions on his business. That is all calculated in the head office, to which accounts are sent every day to be worked out by the clerks employed there. The result may not be called in question by the postmaster.

A sub-office may be knocked up to send a telegram after closing hours, on which there is an extra fee of 2s., or more, out of which a messenger has to be paid to fetch the clerk, the clerk paid for coming to telegraph, and probably porterage paid for delivery at the other end. Therefore the margin of profit is in this case small, though to the public 2s. seems a high fee.

In a sub-office one, two, or three assistants may be necessary. Applicants are more likely to apply for posts in a neighbouring office attached to a grocer's shop, where the three clerks have their meals, but sleep at their own homes, and receive respectively 18s., 16s., or 12s. a week. The hours of work average nine a day, but are in some cases 12. The usual holidays are Sundays, Christmas Day, and Good Friday, in addition to a fortnight in the summer. The clerks take it in turn to be away on Bank Holidays.

Saddlery Trade

Apprenticeship for practical saddler, seven years; wages 5s., rising to 12s. Shorter apprenticeships are becoming more common. Journeyman saddler earns from 25s. to 35s. per week. A small saddlery business may be started on £100 capital. More is often required on account of the long credit frequently prevailing, and the practice of bribing coachmen and grooms to secure and retain wealthy customers is unfortunately common.

The effect of the motor-car upon the saddlery trade is appreciated only by those who know the trade well. The extensive services of motor omnibuses is an additional cause for alarm, already acute from the extensive following of the motor fashion by private owners.

Motors do not, and probably never will, affect the hunting trade, to which, therefore, the efforts of the trade should be directed. If military contracts can be secured, it is often a good thing. The profits are small, but the orders are large and the money certain.

Side lines: Saddler-made purses have a reputation for long life which they deserve, and are not to be despised; but they are given to last too long, and when we hear of one which has stood the strain of daily handling for twenty years, one feels that the benefit has been all with the purchaser and not with the saddler who made and sold the article.

Surgical Instrument Dealers

These are departments of a chemist's business which are often much neglected. The stock required is not large, but it is necessary to have a lady assistant for fitting on ladies' surgical appliances. Often the chemist's wife is available for this purpose, but both qualified and unqualified women chemists are now readily obtainable.

Catheters and bougies and various kinds of syringes are in constant request. Forceps, knives, speculums, and drainage tubes may be mentioned, each of these classes being made in great variety, each for special purposes. Instruments for the ear, eye, mouth, throat, and teeth exist in bewildering variety. Chest-protectors are much required as the winter season approaches. These are made in scarlet or white felt, pine felt, or rabbit skin. When the protectors cover the back as well as the chest, they are known as lung-protectors. Spitting-cups are necessary for bronchial patients; the cups cost from 5s. a dozen.

The uses of indiarubber for surgical appliances are very numerous, chiefly in those cases where impervious articles are desired. Water-proof and air-proof goods are in great demand. Indiarubber urinals for men and women sell at 12s. to 15s. each, but being not much in demand seldom pay to keep in stock. Enema syringes, douche-cans, injection-bottles, spray-producers, breast-exhausters, nipple-shields, and finger-stalls fall into the class of druggists' sundries usually associated with the business of a chemist and druggist.

Belts are used as supports for the abdomen. The measure must be taken with great care as the belt should fit like a glove. The fronts are made flat or round, and it is necessary to give the circumference at three places, and the depth both at the back and front. Ladies' abdominal belts sell at 7s.6d. to 21s. Belts of various kinds are made for gentlemen. The knitted variety is known as a cholera belt; while money belts are often asked for by those going abroad. Chest-expanding braces are needed for women and children; they cost from 4s. to 10s. each.

The measure for artificial limbs is a matter of comparison with the size of the corresponding limb. An artificial leg for amputation above the knee sells at £10 to £15; an artificial arm and hand at about £15. Artificial hands cost from 20s. to 70s. each. Crutches cost from 36s. a dozen pairs, better kinds costing 4s.6d. to 40s. a pair. Leg-irons for deformed legs sell at four to six guineas.

Deaf people require ear-trumpets and conversation tubes. Ear-trumpets in bronzed tin sell at 4s.6d. to 6s., the telescope form from 7s.6d. to 12s. Ear-cornets or resonators are a smaller form; they are made bell- or egg-shaped. Vulcanite trumpets sell at 5s. to 7s.6d. Conversation tubes 3 ft. long cost 2s.6d. and sell at 4s.; but more expensive ones are sold which have ebony mounts and silk-covered tubes. Acoustic fans and audiphones are refinements of hearing apparatus, and sell at from two to three guineas.

Tailors

Working tailor's apprentice serves five years, earning 4s., 5s., 6s., 7s., 8s.6d. a week; journeyman tailor earns 30s. to 35s. a week, but has much idle time. Capital required to start business holding some stock, £30. Shopmen, as distinct from practical tailors, earn 17s. to 30s. a week.

In advertising a tailoring business it is necessary to emphasise the fact that every effort will be made to carry out the customers' wishes; that the talent employed in the cutting and fitting-rooms is such as will enable goods to be supplied that will fit and be stylish; that the materials sold are reliable in both dye and quality; and that the workmanship is such as will give good style and enable the garments to stand the test of wear.

If it is intended to make a special lead of any department, then prominence should be given to it, and this is easily done by issuing charts of fashions, which must, of course, portray the most up-to-date styles. Above all it must be borne in mind that while printer's ink is an excellent advertising medium, it is nevertheless far inferior to the personal recommendation of a pleased customer, so it should be the tailor's aim at all times to send every customer away thoroughly pleased and satisfied.

Telephone Call Offices

Tobacconists, stationers, hairdressers, and indeed many other shopkeepers, can easily arrange — assuming that they are in suitable localities — to make the telephone a source of revenue. This remark applies with special force to London. Any shopkeeper in London may rent from the Post Office or the National Telephone Company a connection on what is called the "message rate".

The subscriber agrees to pay £5 per annum, and deposits 30s., which covers the cost of 360 calls at a penny each. This rate applies to exchanges within the County of London, and the penny fee covers communication all over that area, as for instance from a Central subscriber to a Hampstead or Western subscriber, and with unrestricted communication over both Post Office and National systems. There is no charge for calls received from other subscribers.

A wall instrument should be chosen, as being the least liable to faults. The shopkeeper may procure a swing sign with the legend YOU MAY TELEPHONE FROM HERE or PUBLIC TELEPHONE and have it placed over the door of his shop, and he may then proceed to allow the public to transact their business over the instrument, charging them any fee he may care to fix. In London, the usual fee is twopence.

In some cases, to avoid keeping accounts against the exchange, the call subscriber rents a coin-collecting box at 30s. per annum, and into this the caller is directed by the operator to place a penny on making a call. This plan does not work so well as the first, besides being slower and somewhat complicated.

Toy Merchants
Selling toys requires patience and a pleasant manner. Children are not attracted by the typical business face and bearing. They not unreasonably and quite unconsciously assume that selling toys is as interesting as buying them, and success comes only to those retailers who can win the goodwill of the little folk. Sixpence to many a child is a little fortune, and not to be spent without first weighing the relative merits of many articles. Even parents are difficult to please in this matter, with the result that what appears to be a simple matter is really one calling for no little tact and courteous attention.

In most big centres there are large warehouses where novelties can be seen and stock selected. The chief of these are to be found in Houndsditch, in London. A visit to these centres twice a year will afford better opportunities of replenishing stock than haphazard purchasing from travellers or by post from catalogues, in which the descriptions of the stock are ordinarily more artistically adorned than accurate.

Undertakers
In selecting this business for a career in life there are several special qualifications which a man must possess before he can hope to be successful. He must, first of all, be endowed with an abnormal amount of self-control.

There is no proper apprenticeship in the trade. As a matter of fact, it is seldom that a youth sets out with the deliberate intention of becoming an undertaker. It is looked upon as a dismal calling, and one to be avoided. But it is a very necessary business, and one which, properly cultivated, yields a reasonable commercial return.

The duties of an undertaker are to measure the dead body, to make the coffin, or to get it made, to arrange with the cemetery authorities, to provide the carriages and men, and to accompany the funeral to the grave. There are funeral furnishers, however, who do not come directly into contact with the mourners.

There is a class of men who are coffin-makers pure and simple, and who are neither cabinet-makers nor carpenters. These men do not possess any great skill, and are often chosen more for their appearance and manners, as they have to assist their employers in coffining the body and at the funeral. Coffin-makers are paid from 6d. to 9d. per hour, according to the class of work they can do. There is no uniformity of hours possible, for coffins must be made at any hour necessary.

From a hygienic point of view cremation is regarded by public health authorities as preferable to earth burial, and this form of disposal of dead bodies is slowly gaining in popularity. But there is yet a deal of sentiment to be overcome before cremation can be universally adopted; moreover the cost is prohibitive for people of ordinary means.

In America embalming is a common practice. The process consists in treating the body so as to preserve it in its natural coloration by retarding decomposition. The usual method adopted is to make an incision in the carotid artery, and inject a solution of zinc chloride and salt. This fluid permeates every part of the organism, thus effecting the desired result and without leaving any unsightly traces of the operation. If the body is to be sent abroad or is to be kept for weeks, the quantity of the solution and its strength are increased and various incisions are made. There are several professional embalmers in London with whom undertakers may make arrangements. Their fees to the trade for an ordinary embalming (say preservation for a week) is about £5 5s. plus fares and expenses.

Shopkeeping for Men: Concluding Observations

Fighting the co-operatives
There are several forms of competition — economic growths of the last few decades — which the present-day retailer has to face. One is the co-operative society, which, from the retailer's point of view, has grown to such alarming dimensions in the North of England, and another is the large city stores. We have known flourishing businesses inaugurated cheek by jowl with large co-operative stores. The business done in most co-operative society shops is, at

certain hours of the day, very large, and customers have frequently to wait a very long time before leaving with their wants satisfied. We have known this turned to advantage. A notice, "No waiting here. Immediate attention", has frequently proved an inducement which brought streams of shillings to the till during the hours of congestion next door.

Competition from department stores

To fight the department store is almost as difficult as it is to combat co-operation. The best weapons are a fresh and varied stock, promptness in delivery, and punctuality in attention to details. Some goods should be sold at lower prices than the large stores, and care should be taken to announce the fact.

        Some small shop-keepers are content with their position. So long as his business returns to him a profit sufficient to defray the expenses of a moderately comfortable domestic establishment, and to rear and educate his family fairly well, the average retail shopkeeper eats the bread of thankfulness and, when his appointed time comes, dies in the assurance or hope that the goodwill of his shop will suffice to provide the means of living to those whom he leaves behind. For the man or firm who seeks to spread there are many avenues towards both the upward path of success and the chasm of failure.

Debt collecting

Every shop-keeper has the desire to attain immunity from loss from bad debts, but many neglect elementary precautions that would, if employed, reduce such loss materially. Assuming that repeated applications for payment of a debt have been ignored, there remains for the shop-keeper legal proceedings against the debtor. Some men are so averse from instituting such proceedings that they would rather lose the money owed. This attitude is wrong, and if made a practice, puts a premium on commercial fraud.

Business correspondence

Every business correspondent has had experience of awkward clients, persons whose peculiarities of temperament are evidenced in their communications in the form of ill-chosen and even rude expressions. The most even-tempered man is strongly tempted sometimes to write a hasty reply to a letter of the kind referred to. But the temptation should be resisted, and the answer allowed to wait, when calmer feelings and further consideration will probably suggest a widely different and much more courteous reply. A curt reply, dictated in a fit of temper, has been the immediate cause of many a closed account. A business man cannot afford to indulge in sarcasm at the expense of his customers.

Advertising - be unique

It has been stated that the retailer who does not spend as much money upon advertising as he does upon shop rent is a fool. This is sweeping, but it contains a germ of truth. Never be afraid of being unique. The hoardings, the walls of railway stations, the sides of street buses and tramcars ought to carry, instead of the announcements of soaps, pills, and cocoas, far more advertisements by local traders. The trade papers — and there are several appealing to every class of shopkeeping — contain a good deal of matter that suggests advertising ideas, and the man who would be right up to date should subscribe for every trade paper that appeals to his departments. The few shillings per annum that these cost is well invested money, not merely from the advertising point of view, butt also for the general trade information purveyed in every issue.

Horse and van

The upkeep of a horse and van in a city like London cannot be reckoned at less than 20s. a week. In country places it may be somewhat less, down to 12s. a week in a village. A good van fresh from the works costs £35, but a second-hand one suitable for a new start may be had for half this figure. If cheaper than the latter sum, there is usually something wrong with it, and it often happens that investment in a new vehicle would have proved more economical than the purchase of a second-hand article. Paint, like charity, can be made to cover a multitude of sins. The chief point in buying a second-hand van is to see that the wheels are good.

  The price of a suitable horse varies considerably; £15 must be paid for one, and more, if possible. The sum mentioned may include a spavin and a few sand-cracks, but one cannot have everything for three five-pound notes. If the trader does not aspire to employ animal traction, £10 to £15 will purchase a good covered baker's barrow or a cycle delivery carrier.

Our Millions of Producing Operatives

To show the essential conditions of employment in which our millions of producing operatives labour, the details given in the following pages have been compiled. Such an attempt has never before been made.

Bakers and confectioners
Wages and conditions vary much in different districts. In large factories in London, adult hands receive 30s. per week, and all time beyond 10 hours in any one day is paid for at 50 per cent above ordinary rate. London shop hands are divided into four grades.

Barge builders
Apprenticeship of seven years enforced. Usual wages of 6s. rising to 13s. per week. The union rate of wages for barge building on the Thames is 10d. per hour and 11½d. for overtime. Hours of work, 54 per week.

Basket-makers
Apprenticeship is still the rule in the chief centres when the work is done in factories, but many of the chief baskets are made by "sweated industry", when the wages of the workpeople are barely sufficient to sustain existence. Apprentices to basket-making are perhaps usually the sons of basket-makers, and there is nothing approaching uniformity in apprenticeship wages. Hours are nominally about 56 per week. Bamboo and cane work is chiefly done by foreigners in London who work hard for very little money, a male adult worker averaging perhaps only from 15s. to 20s. per week of 60 to 70 hours. There are a few places where better conditions prevail, but these are limited and confined to high-class work.

Bedstead makers
Apprenticeship uncommon. Boys enter the works at about 15, at an average wage of 8s. per week, rising by successive increases to 15s. at the age of 18. From 18 to 21 the youth usually receives a bonus of 15 per cent on salary in addition to annual increases. At 21 he earns 23s. plus the bonus. The greater part of the trade is in piecework. The hours worked vary from 52 to 54 per week.

Blacksmiths
In the North of England unindentured apprenticeship of five or six years is usual. Boys usually start in the smith's shop as hammer drivers at the age of 14 years. After 12 months as strikers they are promoted to a fire, and work as apprentice smiths up to 21 years of age. The standard rate of wages for blacksmiths is 34s. to 38s. per week, according to the district in which they are employed. Smiths in the coach and wheelwright trades work longer than in other branches, usually 56 hours, and earn less, with no higher rate for overtime.

Bleachers
No branch of this industry would lend itself to apprenticeship. The various processes are in themselves of a simple character and readily acquired. The custom of the trade is that young persons enter the works and gradually pass upwards from one department to another as they grow older. Bleaching starts in what is called the crofthouse, where the grey cloth undergoes a drastic process of washing and bleaching. The cloth proceeds from the croft to various departments to be filled, calendered, beetled, made up, and packed.

Bricklayers
System of apprenticeship is becoming most strict and more generally recognised. Time usually served is seven years, although five and six years are not unknown. Apprentice wages differ. Average is probably 5s. per week for the first year, with an annual increase of 2s.6d. a week. Winter work is hard, and in time of frost ceases altogether. During severe winters workmen may be idle for as long as 12 weeks.

Carpenters and joiners
Machinery and the growth of departmentalism have wrought great changes in the trade. Formerly, five years' apprenticeship and often a heavy premium were required from lads entering the trade. A boy works for three or four years, beginning at 3s. a week to 1d. per hour, and rising annually by ½d. per hour. As an improver he may receive 5d. or 6d. per hour. Large shops, where departmentalism prevails, do not give so good a training as smaller shops. Apprenticeship lasts five to six years. Hours, 48 to 60 per week. Wages 10½d. per hour in London.

Carriage builders
Apprenticeship lasts for seven years, usually beginning at 3s. per week and advancing by 1s. to 2s. increments each year. The wages of adult operatives are from 34s. to 40s. per week of 53 hours. A man is practically worth what he makes himself worth, as machinery is not used to any great extent. Smiths, vicemen, bodymakers, painters and trimmers are in practically constant employment.

Chainmakers
Boys who enter the chainmaking trade are usually the sons of workers. No apprenticeship system proper; boys begin by blowing the bellows in outshops, then go on to form the links, rising to the manufacture of cheap untested chains, and finally becoming skilled workmen. All work is by piece, and the workmen may earn anything between 20s. and 40s. per week. Hours are irregular, but no work is done after 5.30 p.m. in factories. Cradley Heath is the centre of the chainmaking industry. Modern practice tends to introduce machine-forged chains, and the hand forger will find smaller scope for his skill.

Clockmaking
The trade of the clockmaker is not in such a parlous state as that of the watchmaker. Boys entering the trade are not now taught it properly, as attention to an automatic machine has taken the place of skilled knowledge of horology. Wages are usually 8d. to 9d. per hour for 54 hours' work, and machine minders may earn more according to the work put out, so that 1s. per hour is not uncommon.

Clog makers
The apprenticeship system is general; one apprentice to three workmen. Lads serve seven years, or until 21 years of age. Their wages are low during the whole term — starting with about 5s. per week, and finishing with about 13s. per week.

    Adult operatives work about 58 or 60 hours per week, starting work at 8.30 or 9 a.m., but there is no rule regulating the hours. They come and go as they please, and as all work is paid for by the piece, there is no extra overtime payment. Sole makers can earn over 40s. per week, and seatsmen from 27s. to 32s. per week. Wages are always tending upwards, and there has not been one instance of reduction in the last 60 years.

Coal miners

Miners do not technically serve what is understood as an apprenticeship in other trades. In the Northumberland districts lads are paid at the standard rate of 1s.1d. plus 15 per cent per day of 10 hours. Drivers of ponies receive 1s.4d., plus 15 per cent per day. Other "off-hand" boys underground receive from 1s.6d. to 3s.3d. plus 15 per cent per day, according to the class of work upon which they are engaged. Standard wages of pony putters are 3s.2d. plus 15 per cent and of hand putters 4s.8d. plus 15 per cent per day. Hewers with long hours (7¼) earn 5s.2s. plus 15 per cent, and with short hours (6¾) 4s.9½d. plus 15 per cent.

Compositors in the printing trade

Apprenticeship general; length, seven years. Beginning wage varies, usually 4s. to 5s., rising 2s. per week per year. London compositors usually earn 39s. for 52½ hours' work. Overtime paid 3½d. per hour extra for the first three hours, 4d. per hour extra for the next two hours, and 5d. per hour afterwards.

Linotype and monotype machine operators are also taken from the composing-room. The hours are shorter, only 48 per week, and wages begin at 45s. in London. Newspaper work is highly remunerated. Good men can easily earn £3 to £4 per week, and operators of exceptional speed a good deal more.

Cotton spinners and weavers

There is no system of apprenticeship in the cotton trade. For most departments, the operatives need training from early youth as the necessary deftness of the fingers and delicacy of touch can be acquired only during that period. As a rule, they are taken straight from school and employed as "learners". No wage is paid during the period of "learning", but inducements are at present offered in the shape of pocket-money.

After say four, or at most six weeks, the "learner" is put on the duties performed by children or young persons. In spinning mills, these duties are, for girls, back tenting, the average wage for which is about 10s. per week; for boys, little piecing, or "scavenging", as it is called in the Bolton district, the wages for which average about 12s.6d.

Hours of work are 55½ per week — viz. 6 a.m. to 5.30 p.m., less 1½ hours for meals, and 6 a.m. to 12 noon on Saturdays, less ½ hour for meals. There is no recognised overtime worked in the cotton trade, the chief reason being that child labour is so necessary to nearly all departments, and the hours of labour for such are fixed by the Factory Acts.

Wages in the great weaving centres differ, of course, from those in the spinning centres. All weavers, whether men or women, are paid the same piecework rates, which are contained in a list which applies to all Lancashire. Each weaver attends to as many looms as his or her efficiency warrants. It varies from two to six looms, and the earnings range about 6s.6d. or 7s. per loom. In the case of a weaver minding six looms, a helper is needed, who is paid out of the weaver's earnings.

Farriers

In the provinces apprenticeship is common; but in London it is almost unknown and the ranks of the trade are recruited from the provincial inflow. Hours vary from 52 to 61 per week, and a certain amount of Sunday work is often performed. The work is exhausting, and especially when the hours are irregular, as they frequently are, they tell upon the individual.

Furriers

Apprenticeship is not very common. Usually a boy of 15 or 16 is taken to learn the trade, and is paid 10s. per week, rising gradually for three or four years. At the end of this time he is considered an improver, and does general work of a not very responsible character. Then he learns nailing and cutting. A cutter earns from £2 to £3.15s. per week, or even more, and 50 per cent more for overtime.

The hours are 9 a.m. to 6 p.m. from Christmas to Easter; and from Easter to Christmas, 8.30 a.m. to 7 p.m. Saturdays until 1 or 1.30 p.m. There are chances of a smart man becoming a sorter and buyer of goods and blossoming into a fur merchant.

Gasfitters

The conditions generally are the same as those for plumbers. Gasfitters' work is inside to a greater extent than plumbers' work, hence time is not lost by the short day during the winter months as it is in the plumbing trade.

Glaziers
Apprenticeship not uniform, but usual term is five years. Indentured apprentices usually begin at 6s. a week, advancing 2s. per week annually. Unindentured apprentices often earn more then indentured apprentices when they have been some time at the trade. Workmen's hours and wages are not uniform, but the average is about 8½d. an hour in larger towns for a 51-hour week. Overtime is paid at one and a quarter rates.

Jewellers
London is the seat of the better-class jewellery trade and the workmen engaged are largely foreign. Apprenticeship exists but is not general. Departmentalism is seriously affecting the quality of the workmen turned out, and the demand for foreign skilled labour shows no sign of decrease. Ordinary work is paid for at the rate of 7d. to 1s. per hour, and 1s. to 1s.6d. for best work. Workmen who have special skill in modelling and designing may make up to as much as £10 a week. Such men are chiefly Frenchmen.

Gold beating is a poorly remunerated and a dying craft, owing to foreign competition. Wages average only 20s. to 30s. per week. There are no youths entering the trade.

Gold and silver wire drawing is done chiefly by women, who earn up to 13s. per week. There has been much short time lately on account of slackness. Girls learn the trade in about a year after having been taken on as message girls.

Lead workers
Makers of lead pipes and sheets, lead shot and capsules have no apprenticeship. Workmen of extra skill may earn as much as 35s. a week; but the average rate is 24s. to 28s., although some make not more than 20s. Girls are employed in making and decorating lead bottle capsules, earning 7s. to 12s. a week or, if forewomen, 16s.

Lock makers
Apprenticeship used to be general, but it is now obsolete. All locks are now made by piecework, and an expert and expeditious worker may earn twice as much as a clumsy fellow at his elbow. Some men earn not more than 20s. a week, while more skilled comrades will pocket 40s. a week or more, working

at the same terms on identical work. Preparing parts of locks is often done by day workers at 6d. per hour plus 20 per cent. The preparation and parts for common locks is done by youths and girls at about 8s. per week of 54 hours.

Marble and slate masons
The number of apprentices is restricted. Three are usually considered sufficient for a shop of, say, forty men. Apprenticeship lasts five years; wages begin at 5s. per week and rise by 2s. per week annually. Some of the best London shops require a £20 premium from apprentices. Many workmen urge the need for a longer apprenticeship, as it is held that five years is too brief to turn out competent men, and journeymen who have just finished a five years' apprenticeship frequently accept 3d. an hour under workmen's standard wage. Present wage in London is 10½d. per hour for 48½ hours per week.

Masons and stonecutters
In England, apprentices must be 14 years old. They serve seven years, starting wages 1d. per hour for the first year. The average wages are 8d. per hour, except for outside work in winter, when the rate is ½d. higher. Overtime up to 10 p.m. is paid at one and a quarter rate, and from 10 p.m. to 6 a.m. double time. Men required to work more than four miles from the shop are often paid 1d. per hour extra as "lodging money", with fares in addition. Hours of shop work are usually 54 per week.

Painters
Conditions vary considerably. Apprenticeship, often six years, beginning 3s. to 5s. and rising from 12s. to 16s. In London apprenticeship is almost extinct, and where it still prevails it seldom lasts longer than one year. Ship painters work 54 hours. The position of the working painter is not particularly desirable. Three-quarters of the total number have no employment for more than nine or ten months in the year.

Piano makers
The trade is becoming less skilled than formerly on account of the subdivision of labour, and there are no apprentices proper. Boys who wish to learn the trade thoroughly should enter the employment of one of the smaller makers.

Plasterers
Apprenticeship, five years at 5s. per week, rising 2s. each year. Usual rule is one apprentice to two workmen. Workmen, 51 hours per week at 7½d. to 9½d. per hour. Varies in different districts. Overtime, time and a half.

Plumbers
Apprenticeship was formerly for seven years but now five years is common. Premiums of from £5 to £50 sometimes demanded by good firms. Wages begin at 2s.6d. to 5s. per week and rise to from 15s. to 20s. during the last year. Wages for workmen vary from 6d. per hour in some country districts to 11d. per hour in London. The London hours are 47 per week, but in the provinces they are sometimes as many as 56½.

Silk hatters
A seven years' indentured apprenticeship compulsory. Workmen are paid by a complicated piecework scale, and earn 40s. to 60s. a week. From January to June hours are 11 per day and from July to December 9 per day. Saturday work ceases at 1 p.m. No over-time allowed, and breakers of this rule are fined 6d. for every five minutes by the workmen's union.

Umbrella makers
No indentured apprenticeship, but competence is considered to be attained only after eight or nine years' experience. Standard wages for frame makers are 30s. per week, for cutters 33s., and for finishers 30s. per week. The hours are 55 per week and overtime is paid at one and a quarter rates.

Watchmakers
Terms of apprenticeship as under Jewellers, but tendency is to reduce the time served. The two trades are usually allied. Technical instruction in horology given at Horological Institute, London, both to attending students and to learners by correspondence. The English watch trade has gone and no youths are entering it. Most of the workmen now in it are old men who learned the craft in its flourishing days. Wages are by piecework and 40s. to 60s. is the rule for men of skill, but this is little more than half what was formerly a common remuneration.

POSTSCRIPT: Emigration to the Colonies

This is a fitting place for a word to those who think about tempting fortune by embarking upon a commercial career in one of the Colonies. Opportunity in a rapidly expanding country with a wide future before it is much more frequent, and the prospect of success much greater, than in this overcrowded competition-ridden homeland.

New countries are essentially the countries for young men. There is not the weary waiting for dead men's shoes; and when opportunity comes, its hands are heavier with material gifts. Further, the fact that so many indifferent men — often wasters and incompetents — seek these far countries in search of riches or livelihood which they have been unable to find at home magnifies the chances of success to the really competent, energetic man who matches himself against them.

No one should set up business in the Colonies or in a foreign country without having had business experience in the country. He must find employment, gain experience, and then wait a favourable chance.

Sometimes positions abroad may be obtained before leaving home. When men are engaged in this country for such situations they are often required to enter into an agreement for a term of years — usually three — and have their passage paid. This practice is less common than it was, but it still prevails. It is not a good one. The new man usually finds that, although he has taken a seemingly remunerative position, viewed from the British wage standard, the remuneration which he has agreed to accept is less than that ruling in the market whither he has gone. He is tied up for the term of engagement, and cannot therefore improve his position should opportunity offer. He is also assisting to spoil the market in his new home. The two-pounds-a-week shop assistant in England is worth £25 a month in Johannesburg and about as much in Winnipeg. And he need not think that he will be able to save the difference. The higher price of necessaries and luxuries makes that impossible.

It is always better for the shopman emigrant, if he is a good man, to pay his own fare and begin employment upon the understanding that he can leave at reasonable notice. If he is a man of inferior quality, he will be wise, however, to engage himself for a term of years if he can, otherwise he would find himself a member of the army of the unemployed, for Colonial business men do not keep poor servants long if there is a chance to replace them.

PART TWO:
WHAT SHALL WE DO WITH OUR GIRLS?

The Lady Shopkeeper

Baby-linen outfitters
The vending of baby clothes is essentially a woman's occupation. It has many attractions for womankind, and especially for those who have known the joys of motherhood. It is an ideal occupation for a widow with only a small capital, and if she has any business ability, it can be made not only the means of a livelihood, but even of securing a competency. Many married women with business aspirations start a baby-linen shop in order to augment the income of a delicate or otherwise unfortunate husband, and the woman with tact, taste, and ability to "use her hands" invariably succeeds.

With a sum of £100 to £150 in hand, a fairly advantageous start may be made, the neighbourhood selected being, for preference, a popular residential one. A main street is not essential, unless the adventuress has ambitions beyond a merely family business. The trade is primarily a personal one, and a suitable shop should be chosen in a neighbourhood where mothers and children abound.

Accessories: There are many little things incidental to the business. These all tend to swell the profits; they cost little and look imposing. First may be mentioned macintosh goods, such as aprons for the nurse, accouchment sheets, diapers for the mother, sponge-bags and pilches.

The window should be lightly dressed, with not too many articles displayed, and it should be dressed daily. Include a few dummy children arranged in all their glory, placed at the back. Hoods, dresses, and coats could be dotted here and there about the shop on stands.

Dressmakers
Although at the present day the field of commercial enterprise offers many and varied opportunities to the woman who is desirous of earning her living — and practically any form of employment is open to her — still, with few exceptions, women workers have confined themselves to the businesses in which they participate with their own hands, such as dressmaking, millinery,

cookery, and laundry-work, and the majority of them have achieved success as dressmakers.

The past twenty years or so have also witnessed the entry of society women into the commercial world, and in most cases they have proved themselves capable and efficient. It is one of the signs of the times that an aptitude for business, and the capacity for success in trade, should no longer be looked upon as evidences of plebeian origin and the peculiar attributes of the middle or lower classes, but are now envied qualities in many clever, hard-working women of good birth and recognised social position, who have elected to turn those talents to account in the domain of dress or millinery.

To start a high-class dressmaking business in London, it would be necessary to have at least £1000 capital, especially if the locality chosen be in a West End neighbourhood, as such a position would entail high rent; and a fashionable dressmaker in town is always supposed to give three months' credit, and is frequently obliged to give six months.

It would be unwise for anyone to start for herself without having at least three years' experience with a good firm. She should be an accurate cutter and fitter, possessing the artistic faculty to some extent, and having a correct eye for colour; should have a practical knowledge of trimmings, laces, etc; and thoroughly understand the intricacies of buying and selling, the preparation of estimates, and all the details necessary to the successful management of a business. A good system of bookkeeping is most important.

Milliner

Two years' apprenticeship and no wages paid. A premium of £10 to £20 is often required. Assistants earn from £10 to £30 a year. Capital required to start, £100; more if extended credit is given.

Locality and position will probably depend upon the amount of capital available. The risk of failure is often less in a fashionable seaside resort, or a provincial town, than in London, where expenses are so heavy, and where competition is so keen. Too much care cannot be given to the artistic fitting up and furnishing of the rooms. The fashionable London milliner usually trades under a fancy name, such as "Monica", "Dolly Varden", or "Lucile". Her showrooms are like handsomely appointed and luxurious drawing rooms, with the softest of carpets, choice bric-a-brac, and Louis Quinze furniture; very little is there to show any connection with millinery, except a few hats, laid here and there, as if by accident, a few more on stands in the corners of the room, and deep oak drawers running round the walls.

The most private and expensive milliners are usually established up one or two flights of stairs, or, if on the ground floor, not more than two or three models are permitted to be exposed to the vulgar gaze, all exclusive designs being jealously hidden away under folds of tissue paper in boxes or drawers.

Unless the West End milliner starts with a large connection, she will obviously require a substantial sum for advertising, as her windows count for little or nothing in this respect.

In addition to the usual stock in trade, ready-made blouses, lace, ruffles, scarves, and lingerie and corsets are frequently sold by milliners. This is more than ever the case since the advent of the motor-car, which is said to be ruining the millinery trade. Where formerly four or five hats would have been sold, nowadays only one, and a few cheap motor caps and veils will be considered sufficient.

One experienced assistant, costing from 16s. to 21s. a week, with two or three improvers at about 6s., will probably be sufficient hands to begin with, and when increase of business justifies the engagement of another assistant she should, if possible, be a Frenchwoman.

In addition to the ordinary fashion journal and circular advertising, any plan which might suggest itself as likely to bring people to the show-room should be tried. In one case, a good connection was established in a very short time chiefly owing to the fact that afternoon tea was served to customers every day. The particular premises referred to happened to be unusually suitable, and the outlay and trouble involved were trifling, while the increase of custom was remarkable.

It is all-important to remember that the great object, especially of the beginner, is not so much to sell a hat as to please the customer and bring her back to the shop, probably with a friend next time. Whether living in town or country, frequent trips to Paris should be made.

Sweet Sellers

If the beginner has about £50 capital she may make a very creditable start. Of course, this is a small amount, and the beginning would be humble. A good middle-class neighbourhood, and a small shop with living-rooms attached, would be selected by the young wife or spinster with ambition, taste, and the capital named.

A handy husband or male friend could fit up and stain a few shelves around the shop and in the window. A counter, a pair of scales, weights, a scoop, and a gross or two of paper bags of different sizes would not cost more than a few pounds. Neatness, brightness, and, above all, cleanliness are essential, but the clever woman would find it little trouble to adorn the shelves with fancy paper or other drapery, and so make the place attractive. Receptacles for the goods are not really necessary, for the manufacturers send out their productions in good bottles, and other containers, with attractive labels. These bottles are charged for when sent out, but the charge is credited when the bottles are returned empty. Some manufacturers even supply ornamental cases and dainty show-bottles free on loan to advertise their wares.

Small quantities and much variety should be the rule, for in nothing is the public taste so peculiar and varied as in sweets. Therefore, give the public variety, and never let the window be too great a trouble. Let the stock be carefully watched and arranged so that the old is got rid of before the new is begun upon. If in a busy thoroughfare, near a railway station, theatre, or place of amusement, it is essential that packets of sweets be always kept ready to be picked up, for travellers and amusement seekers have not usually much time to waste in fastidious selection.

An endeavour should be made by issuing leaflets, displaying special lines, and so forth, to secure a reputation for selling better caramels, or chocolates, or fondants, or what not, at the same price as competitors. This reputation once established, people will go a long way to get your particular speciality, and they should be made to feel that you are glad to see them.

Daintiness — that peculiar attribute of womankind — is even more essential than painful neatness and rigid cleanliness. It is not always necessary to show full packets of sweets, for many manufacturers supply good customers with dummies, and there are plenty of artistic showcards to be obtained free of charge from manufacturers to enliven any spare wall space there may be. Only stock reliable goods; the "cheap and nasty" trade is not worth the candle.

Lady Post Office Clerks

A girl desirous of becoming a clerk in a sub post-office has no competitive examination — in fact, no examination whatever to encounter. She comes into the office as a learner without salary. If she proves capable, after a time she receives a small salary. Every branch of the work has to be mastered by her. Advertisements for such learners will frequently be found in, for instance, the "Christian World". The sub-agent is not allowed to take premiums with his employees.

In a country office the junior clerk may be wanted to keep the books of the business or perform housework; not, however, in a London sub-office. She occasionally assists in a light business when the postal business is slack; but all such additional work is discountenanced by the officials, who sometimes institute inquiries respecting this matter.

It will be readily understood that it is an advantage to a postmaster to employ one or more members of his own family in the post-office, especially in country districts. The daughters often naturally slip into such vacant posts.

Principal Careers for Women

Recent years have witnessed the entry of women into many fields formerly deemed to be exclusively for men. These details regarding some of the principal careers for women may help to solve the problem "What shall we do with our girls?"

Accountants
For women with an aptitude for figures, there are openings as accountants and auditors. The training is the same as for men. The candidate should be sufficiently well educated to pass the preliminary examination of the Institute of Chartered Accountants, although membership of that body is still denied to women. She should be articled to an accountant for five years, and pass the three prescribed examinations. The cost of training is from £100. Age limit from 18 to 21. Women are frequently employed to audit the accounts in girls' schools and colleges.

Bookbinding
This is work which may often be done by women in their own homes. A thorough training is necessary, as well as artistic instincts. A twelve months' course of training costs about £70. It is fairly remunerative.

Chromo-lithography
Three years are necessary to become fully acquainted with the work. There are many openings both at home and in the Colonies for workers who are well qualified. Salaries average from 20s. to 35s. a week.

Church
In the United States hundreds of women have been ordained, and are practising as ministers, but there are, so far, no openings of the kind in the United Kingdom, although one lady has recently been appointed pastor of a church in a provincial town. A number of women find employment as church workers, but this work is never well paid. Bible women, when trained at one of the homes in connection with various charitable organisations, are paid from £40 to £60 a year. The Church Army Mission nurses are paid 14s. a week, with lodging.

Civil service

An increasing number of women find employment as clerks in the Civil Service, chiefly in the various branches of the Post Office. Posts are obtained by open competitive examination, in which a high standard of proficiency must be attained, as competition is very keen. The examination is in the usual English subjects and two foreign languages. Fee 7s.6d. The age limit for women clerks is from 18 to 20, salary to begin £55, rising to £100 per annum. One month's holiday is given, and a pension or gratuity on resignation. For girl clerks, the age is from 16 to 18, and the beginning salary £35. At the end of two years they may be promoted, if competent, to the rank of women clerks, starting at a salary of £55.

Female sorters in the Post Office pass an examination in English. Age limit 15 to 18. Salary begins at 12s. a week and rises to 21s.6d. Between the ages of 18 and 25 sorters may enter the open competitive examinations for women clerks. The security of tenure, short working hours, and length of holidays, together with the prospect of a pension, make this a very desirable career for women.

Commercial travellers

A few women are employed as commercial travellers in England, and a much greater number are doing well as such in the United States. The posts obtained in this country are chiefly in connection with the drapery trade, and are usually given to employees who have shown special ability and are well acquainted with the business of their firm.

Dairy work

The training at one of the dairy schools recognised by the Board of Education lasts from six to twelve months, and costs about £1 to 30s. a week, including board and residence. Salaries paid to dairy teachers under the county councils range from £1.5s. to £3 a week. Superintendents of dairies on private estates are paid from £25 to £60 a year with board and residence.

Dentistry

There are few women dentists to be found in England, although numbers are practising in the States and Canada. The Royal College of Surgeons of Dublin and Edinburgh grant the diploma in Dental Surgery to women, who may then be registered for practice by the Medical Council. The cost of training is somewhat less than for medicine.

Dispensers

The highest training of women dispensers consists of a three years' apprenticeship to a qualified chemist, to whom a fee of from £50 to £70 may in some cases have to be paid. Training and examinations are as for men. Women have obtained posts as dispensers in hospitals and other institutions at from £80 to £150 per annum. There are also openings as dispensers to medical men, who often accept the certificate of the Apothecaries' Assistants' Examination, together with a course at a school of Pharmacy, as sufficient qualification. The average tuition fee for a three months' course at a school of Pharmacy is about ten guineas.

Domestic science

Technical Education in Domestic Science is a development of quite recent years, and the profession of domestic science teacher is one which is very suitable for an active woman of good education. Training lasts about two years; the cost of the complete course varies from £18.18s. to £55. Instruction in cookery, laundry work, dressmaking, millinery and hygiene is given in schools of cookery throughout the country, also in both elementary and secondary schools. Salaries of teachers for these posts range from £70 to £250 a year. There are also posts obtainable under borough councils, and sometimes particularly good colonial appointments are offered to domestic science teachers trained in England.

Dressmaking

There are always plenty of openings for clever women in dressmaking. Apprenticeship lasts two years. In a good house the premium, if indoors, is usually from £60 to £100, and, if the apprentice lives at home, about £30 to £50. On expiry of apprenticeship a post is usually taken as improver for about six months, when assistants' posts may be obtained at from 10s. to 16s. a week, rising in the case of a good worker to £2 a week. A really first-rate fitter can obtain £5 a week. Women who mean to start in business as dressmakers should spend some months at the practical part of the work. To start in London at least £1000 capital would be necessary, as credit must be given.

Florists

Apprenticeship is usually for three years. During part of this time wages of 3s. to 5s. a week are paid. Afterwards assistants may earn from 15s. to 30s. a week. Premiums of from £5 to £30 are usually paid for learning florists' work.

Gardening

A course of instruction at a horticultural college such as that at Swanley or the Lady Warwick College, Reading, usually lasts from two to three years. Fees are from £70 to £80 a year, including board and residence. Instruction is given in horticultural science, flower, fruit, and vegetable growing (out of doors and under glass), market work, packing, and storing. Dairy work, poultry farming, and bee-keeping are extras. When trained, some students obtain positions as lecturers and teachers. Lady gardeners are seldom paid more than £1 a week to begin with. They frequently take resident places as companion-gardener to some lady. To start in business as a market gardener it is necessary to have at least £900 capital.

Hairdressing

In the opinion of some hairdressers there are openings for women in this business. The term of apprenticeship is two years. When the various branches of the work are thoroughly mastered, an assistant can command from 15s. to 35s. a week, usually with a percentage on all articles sold.

Hygiene

There are many well-paid appointments open to educated women who are trained in hygiene. A certificate may be obtained from Bedford College, London, by students who pass the examination held at the end of one year's course in scientific and practical hygiene. The fee is 27 guineas. A shorter and less expensive course may be obtained at the National Health Society, Berners Street, London. The fees there are 15 guineas for six months. For women so qualified, posts have been held as Factory Inspectors, Sanitary Inspectors, Lecturers under the County Councils, and Inspectors under the Shop Hours Act.

Illustrating and fashion-plate drawings
Many women who have received an art training can command good salaries as illustrators of books, magazines and ladies' papers. This is a profession which is not overcrowded. Women who desire employment of this kind should send sets of specimen sketches to the editors of some of the illustrated papers.

Indexing
Openings for work of this kind are always increasing. Indexing is a lucrative employment suitable for well-educated women. The training under an experienced indexer lasts from six to nine months, and the fees are from 15 guineas. Women indexers have recently been appointed by the London County Council. The work can be done at home. Charges range from £2.2s. to £4.4s. per thousand entries.

Journalism
The prospects for women in journalism are fairly good. Payment for special or occasional contributions is equal to that of men, although for regular reporting work women are paid less. Women are also handicapped at the outset by their inability to obtain the thorough routine training which is usually gone through by men, but, given a capacity for hard work, they frequently achieve success.

Laundry work
There is a steadily growing demand for thoroughly well-trained women in laundry-work, both as actual laundresses and as superintendents or manageresses of laundries. The course of training for manageresses in a good laundry usually lasts from three to six months. The fees are from £5 to £10. When the training is completed, if the pupil is thoroughly competent, she may obtain a position as forewoman or assistant manageress at a salary of from £1 to £2.10s. a week. The hours of work are long, being usually from 8 a.m. to 8 p.m., and the work is hard. Manageresses are paid from £2 up to £5 a week.

Librarians
There are not so many openings for women as librarians in this country as in

the United States or Canada, nor are the salaries paid in England sufficiently remunerative to induce women of good education to take up what would otherwise be suitable and congenial work. The best plan to pursue in order to become a librarian is to attend the classes at the London School of Economics and enter for the Examination of the Library Association. The average earnings of a woman assistant in our public libraries is £50 a year. Head librarians are paid £100.

Medicine

Women who desire to qualify as medical practitioners are subject to the Regulations of the General Medical Council in the same way as men. Women are admitted to medical degrees and diplomas equally with men, by the examining bodies of most British Universities, with the exception of Oxford and Cambridge. Posts are open to women doctors in the Post Office, and under the London County Council; also in connection with many hospitals and dispensaries throughout the country. Many women are earning good incomes in private practice in Great Britain, while, owing to the fact that no man can enter the zenanas of the high-caste Hindoo, India offers a wide field of labour. Appointments are open both under Government and in connection with some of the various missionary bodies, the Dufferin Fund, etc.

Millinery

Apprenticeship lasts two years; at the end of first year, wages about 5s. weekly. Assistants in wholesale milliners receive from 12s. to 30s. a week. In the West End shops engagements are often for the season only, when a very experienced hand can command from £2 to £4 or £5 a week. To start in business in London about £400 capital is necessary, also technical training and a taste for the work. For such women the prospects of success are good.

Needlework - Art

At the Royal School Of Art Needlework, South Kensington, training lasts two or three years. Fees for two years' certificate course £20 a year, and for three years' diploma course £10 a year. Hand embroidery, etc., is taught to amateurs. Fee for six lessons, 21s. to 30s. There are many other schools of embroidery in London and the provinces. There is a fair demand for work of this kind in connection with churches. It also commends itself to some women as being work which can frequently be done at home.

Nursing

Hospital nurses receive a training of three years in a hospital to which the average age of admission is from 23 to 30. Some hospitals require a fee of from £10 to £50. Probationers are usually paid from £8 to £15 a year with uniform. When the period of training is over the majority of nurses take up private work, usually joining one of the Co-operative Associations of Nurses. In these societies the nurses retain their own fees, only deducting an agreed percentage for expenses. Their salaries average from £72 to £110 per annum.

Private nursing may also be undertaken for an institution at a fixed yearly salary, ranging from £20 to £40, with uniform, board and residence. Nurses who join Queen Alexandra's Imperial Military Nursing Service, for work at home and abroad, are paid from £40, in addition to quarters, board, allowance, etc. Sisters receive £50 to £65, Matrons, £75 to £105, and the Matron-in-chief from £300 to £350. They also receive a pension upon retirement. Age for appointment from 25 to 35.

In the Naval Hospitals head sisters are paid £125 to £160 in addition to quarters and uniform. Nursing sisters receive from £37.10s. to £50, with board allowance of 15s. a week. District nurses in London or the Provinces are usually trained for two years in a general hospital, and six months in a district nursing home. Salaries from £26 per annum, with everything found.

The training of maternity nurses is usually from three to six months in a maternity hospital or infirmary. Fees for this are usually £10 to £26. The Obstetrical Society of London holds examinations four times yearly, at which certificates are granted to successful candidates. Fee, 21s. A maternity nurse's fee varies from £6.6s. to £21 for a case.

Photography

A course of instruction in photography at the Regent Street Polytechnic costs £52.10s., in addition to which a student should work for a few months as a pupil in some good studio. To start in business in London at least £500 capital would be necessary, although considerably less would suffice for the Provinces. Retouchers in photographic studios may be paid from 25s. to 40s. a week. For working up, 17s.6d. to £2.10s. a week.

Physical training

There appears to be a wide and, so far, unfilled field for women of good physique who are thoroughly trained gymnastic teachers. The course should extend over two years, and costs from £50 to £100, exclusive of living, or as resident pupil at the Physical Training College, from £90 a year. Resident teachers in schools are paid from £40 to £50, non-resident teachers from £100.

Pottery workers
There are a large number of women workers in potteries, mostly helpers, who finish the work of the men. Such women are paid 12s. to 15s. per week. Some women work light machines and earn from 20s. to 25s. per week.

Printing
Apprenticeship lasts for three or four years, but wages begin after about six months. At the Women's Printing Society a premium of £5 is paid, and a small weekly wage is received from the start. The average rate of pay is 24s. a week, but it sometimes rises to 34s. Women compositors who can spell well seldom fail to find work.

Sanitary inspectors
The number of appointments open to women under the County Councils is steadily increasing, and the work which has been done by those already appointed has proved satisfactory. The age limit for London applicants is from 25 to 40, and the requisite qualification is the certificate of the Sanitary Inspectors' Examination Board; for the provinces the Sanitary Institute Certificate is accepted. Salaries vary from £80 to £110 per annum, and rise to a maximum of £150.

Secretarial and clerical work
Women who, in addition to a sound English education, have undergone a special business training in typewriting, shorthand and book-keeping, can obtain posts at from 30s. to £2 a week. If to these qualifications a knowledge of commercial French and German is added, salaries may rise to £3 a week.

Shop assistants
Women shop assistants are chiefly to be found in the drapery trade. Age of entering is usually 14 to 16. In the better class shops a premium of from £20

to £30 is often paid. After three years an assistant receives from £12 to £20 a year indoors, rising in the first-class shops to £70, and, in the case of buyers and heads of departments, to £150 a year. A commission on sales is also given in many shops. The hours are long and the work tiring, and, on the whole, the average wages are less than in other occupations.

Teaching
This profession is one of the few which are not over-stocked. High-school teachers undergo a long and expensive training, usually taking a University degree. Salaries of assistants in a public school are from £50 to £80, with board and residence. Non-resident teachers from £80. In a large private school senior assistants may rise to £140 per annum. Head mistresses of high schools are paid from £180 to £700 a year.

Kindergarten teachers should spend from two to three years in a training college which prepares them for the National Froebel Union Examinations. For teachers so qualified, salaries range from £50 to £100 a year.

PART THREE: UPSTAIRS, DOWNSTAIRS
Duties of Domestic Servants, Great and Small

Butler
The butler is the chief manservant in the household, except in the case of a few wealthy families where a very large retinue of menservants is kept, at their head being the house-steward and chamberlain. All the menservants whose duties are executed indoors live in the house; those whose duties are concerned with outdoor work, such as the gardeners and the coachman, etc., live out of the house.

Certain indoor servants have special privileges connected with their duties. For example, the valet will have little expense connected with his own wardrobe, since he has no livery, and can therefore wear his master's discarded clothes.

The butler, together with the housekeeper, takes precedence over all the other servants. Besides being expected to superintend the other menservants, he has charge of all the valuable articles in daily use, and he is entirely responsible for the management of the wine-cellar. It is therefore obvious that the moral integrity of the butler should be above suspicion. The head-butler's wages vary considerably with different localities, ranging from £60 to £80 per annum.

Housekeeper
The housekeeper is the immediate representative of her mistress. She must supervise the conditions of the servants' lives, seeing that each in turn gets reasonable time for rest, recreation, and exercise, and that the various duties are fairly apportioned.

Although the housekeeper's room is a sanctum, this room should not be far removed from the servants' hall and kitchen. It should be sufficiently near for the housekeeper to have every opportunity of seeing that all is satisfactory in these other rooms; but, on the other hand, it should not be so near that the servants feel an uncomfortable sense of restraint. Servants dislike nothing so much as the idea that they are being "spied on" and petty deceptions and deceit are more than likely to be bred by a system of espionage. A tactful housekeeper will make it evident that she is quite ready to detect wrongdoing or neglect of duty without making her attitude annoyingly aggressive. The ideal housekeeper should endeavour to promote a good tone among the domestics of her household. Her love of cleanliness and order should make itself felt in her organisation and control of the work of the household.

The disposal of a considerable amount of money devolves upon the housekeeper, and she must keep a record of all money that passes through her hands. The housekeeper's accounts should be carefully kept and balanced by the master or mistress at stated intervals. This examination is most desirable and satisfactory to all parties concerned.

The housekeeper must take the greatest care to preserve her own dignity and authority in her dealings with the servants of the household. In the exercise of her duties, the housekeeper should avoid all semblance of being overbearing and exacting, but she should never lose sight of the dignity and responsibility of her position.

The housekeeper's salary will depend much on the conditions under which she is engaged, varying from about £20 to £50, or more in large households.

Valet

The valet is the personal attendant of the master, and his duties consist in looking after his comfort and well-being. The valet has exceptional opportunities of showing his loyalty and zeal in serving his master. He must also possess no small amount of tact and patience, and be able to bear petty annoyances and retain his good temper and respectful manner, even on occasions when his master may be overbearing and irritating.

A good valet will always maintain a respectful demeanour, never allowing himself to lapse into undesirable familiarity. The valet must be absolutely trustworthy. He should be very careful in his conversation in the housekeeper's room, and should never repeat any private family matter which has come to his notice, or which he may accidentally learn in his confidential position. In the matter of his own personal appearance, the valet should take pains to be neat and well-dressed. He never wears a livery, but he is, as a rule, the recipient of the clothes his master no longer cares to wear.

The valet's first duty will be to see that his master's dressing-room has been properly swept and dusted by the housemaid. He should then put all his master's clothing in readiness. Soap, towels, and brushes should be in their proper places. When the master does not shave himself, the valet must be competent to perform the operation.

The servant should also be skilled as a hairdresser, since he will have to brush and arrange his master's hair, and should he possess beard or moustache, these must also be given attention. While the master is dressing, the valet should be in attendance, handing him in turn each article he requires, and adjusting his necktie, etc.

He must find time to keep his master's wardrobe in good order, see that his clothes are well brushed and all stains removed, and his silk hat ironed when necessary. He should also see that the master's toilet is irreproachable, and that all necessary repairs are executed.

During the absence of the master, the valet has not very many duties to perform; but he should be in readiness to wait on his master at all times, and particularly when dressing for dinner. Should he be in attendance on an elderly master, he may be required to give rather closer personal attendance, such as sleeping in an adjoining ante-chamber, accompanying his master out of doors, etc. He may also be required to wait at table, in which case he will stand behind his master's chair and confine his whole attention to administering to his wants.

Sometimes the valet is required to travel with his master. In this case he will doubtless be more or less responsible for looking out routes, taking the tickets, and securing a comfortable seat. He may be required to get tea or newspapers, and he is also responsible for the luggage. He must see that it is properly labelled and put in the van, and keep his master's dressing-case, or bag, under his personal supervision in his own carriage.

Lady's-Maid
The lady's-maid ranks with the valet, and she takes her meals with him, together with the butler, in the housekeeper's room. Her duties bring her into personal contact with her mistress, and it is important that she should possess certain mental and moral qualities to fit her for the work. She should have both tact and patience, and be able to exercise forbearance and self-control should her mistress be unreasonable and capricious. She should never repeat to the other servants anything that may come to her ears, and she should take

care that information of a private character, which may accidentally become known to her, is not repeated.

The lady's-maid's first duty will be to make preparations for her mistress's toilet. She should then, at the appointed time, call her mistress, give her her tea, pull up the blinds, and close the windows. The lady's-maid then goes downstairs to her own breakfast, and her mistress will ring when she is ready for her.

It is of the utmost importance that the lady's-maid should be skilful in dressing hair. If she can obtain some lessons from a good hairdresser she will find them invaluable. Having helped her mistress to dress, the lady's-maid's duties will vary. In all probability she will be responsible for the bedroom and dressing-room. Every particle of dust must be removed, the ornaments dusted, glass and silver ornaments polished, and the dressing-mirror and handglass cleaned. The silver will need particular attention, especially in a town where the fog and smoke will quickly blacken it. The lady's-maid should study her mistress's personal likes in all these details, and do her best to please her in every way.

She should then examine the dresses that her mistress will wear later in the day, and put them out in readiness for use. All discarded dresses, after a short interval for airing, are replaced in the wardrobe. In the matter of mending, she should take charge of everything except stockings and woollen underwear before it goes to the laundry. A small rent will become larger if not mended before the garment is washed. Then, if the mistress prefers narrow, coloured ribbons to tapes in her underwear, the lady's-maid should remove these, and also fragile lace, before sending the article to the laundry; wash them carefully herself, and replace them afterwards.

Many ladies take their maids with them when paying visits. During the journey the maid will probably travel in an adjoining compartment, and should be in readiness to wait on her mistress should there be any changes or long waits at intermediate stations. During the visit her duties will be much the same as those which devolve upon her at home. She will take her meals in the housekeeper's room, where the need for reticence on her mistress's concerns is, of course, even greater than at home.

Footman
The duties of the footman vary considerably, according to whether he works

single-handed or whether there are other footmen working under him. Where others are kept the head footman works in conjunction with the butler. If a valet is not kept, he will doubtless be required to give a certain amount of personal attendance on his master. If there are visitors in the house who have not brought their own valets, he will probably be called upon to give them similar personal attendance.

Certain physical characteristics are generally required in a good footman, such as fair height and good carriage. He may often be sent on messages, or with notes, and should restrain his curiosity as to their purport, and take only such time as is necessary for their delivery. In bringing a note or card to his mistress he should offer it on a salver. In answering the door he should announce visitors distinctly by name. Then in opening the front door for departing guests he should close the carriage door, unless they are accompanied by a footman. The front door should not be closed until the visitors are a short distance from the house.

General Manservant
The single manservant does not wear livery, but his duties combine the most important items of the work of a butler, footman, and valet. He should rise early, and get such work as boot and knife cleaning finished before breakfast. He should see that his master's clothes are brushed, and that hot water is in readiness in the dressing-room. He should then take his own breakfast, and afterwards set that of the household. After he has put the hot dishes on the table, he will probably not be required to wait at table, but may withdraw and begin to busy himself with the morning's task. This may be plate-cleaning, etc.; and he will have to answer the front door.

He will then set the luncheon, and attend at that meal until he is dismissed from the room, when he may retire and take his own dinner. After luncheon he will clear the tables, clean and wash the plate and glass used, and in the afternoon he will generally answer the front-door bell, or go out with the carriage. In the evening his duties will include the laying of the dinner-table. He may be assisted by the parlour-maid, and also in the waiting at table during this meal. After dinner he will clear away, either unaided or assisted as before, and a little later bring in the coffee.

Page and Houseboy

In the case of professional men, it is almost a necessity for a page to be kept whose almost exclusive duty is to answer the front-door bell. In other cases a boy is kept who does not wear livery, nor appear beyond the kitchen precincts. The chief work of the houseboy is to perform tasks which are too heavy for the maidservants. For example, he will bring in coal, clean the knives and boots, and in general make himself useful to the cook and housemaid.

Coachman

The coachman is head of the stables, and should have a wide experience in dealing with horses. He should be skilful in driving, and able to decide wisely in matters concerning the exercise and feeding of the horses entrusted to him. He will probably be required to assist in their choice, and so should be a judge of horseflesh. He should avoid letting his horses get into lazy habits, but at the same time he must not over-drive them.

He should see, before driving up to the front door to fetch his mistress, that everything connected with both carriage and horses is well-arranged and in order. He is not expected to descend from the box, even should no other manservant accompany the carriage, for the ladies can open the door from the inside themselves.

Groom

The chief duty of a groom is to look after the horses, and to see they are in condition. When they are not working regularly they will need to be exercised every day. Each horse will need three meals a day. The groom must be an early riser, for at 6 a.m. or earlier he will have to set about the preparation for the first meal. The groom should be on the alert to see that the shoes of his horses are in good condition. It is well not to attempt much work immediately after a horse has been re-shod. Every day, after exercise, the horses' feet should be washed in water and then well dried with a brush.

Stablemen

The cleaning of the stables is in the hands of the stablemen. Each day the stables should be thoroughly swept, and then washed, buckets of water and stiff brooms being necessary for the process. If this is in any way neglected the results are very disastrous to the freshness and neatness of the stable.

Fresh straw should be placed under the horses directly it is needed.

The carriage should be freed from mud before it hardens and dries. Plenty of water should be thrown over it, and a mop used to clean every crevice. The whole of the interior should be brushed and dusted, the foot-rug taken out and shaken, and the window-glass cleaned and polished.

Gardener

In a large estate the head-gardener will probably be allotted a small house, which privilege is also enjoyed by the coachman. His duties will, to a large extent, consist of organising the work of the men under him. A man may be very deft in one direction and equally clumsy in another, and the head-gardener should see that each man's talents are made the most of in allotting the various tasks.

The head-gardener will be responsible for the supply of fruit and vegetables for the house. One of his privileges is a free supply of such food to his own table; he is also justified in receiving certain commissions from seed merchants, provided that he does not order from a particular firm merely to secure a large commission.

Cook

The cook is the chief of the servants who take their meals in the servants' hall. A punctual cook adds much to the comfort of the household. Her energy is a good example to her fellow-servants.

A good cook is economical in her treatment of food. No scraps are wasted, and she will arrange that food is not allowed to get stale or turn sour. To secure this end it is important that she should examine her larder every day. The cook should go daily through her household supplies to see that no important article is missing. She should keep a slate in some accessible corner of the kitchen, on which to record any deficiency directly she notice it.

Neatness should be the keynote of a cook's attire. Many cooks wear two aprons - a small neat one, and a larger one which practically covers the whole skirt. The upper apron protects the one underneath, and can be quickly removed should the cook need, say, to answer the door.

Kitchenmaid

The kitchen, or scullery maid, does the dirtier part of the kitchen work, leaving the cook more freedom to pursue her culinary duties. The kitchenmaid will probably be entirely responsible for the preparation and serving of her fellow-servants' meals. The exact duties of the kitchenmaid can hardly be defined. They vary in different households, and the requirements and individual wishes of each particular cook determine whether the position of kitchenmaid is altogether desirable and pleasant.

Housemaid

The housemaid should possess a love of order and of punctuality. In a large establishment the upper-housemaid will have only very light duties to perform, but her responsibilities will be fairly heavy, for she will have to superintend the work of the other housemaids. The drawing-room will be under her particular care. In small households, where there are many grown-up daughters and few servants, the care of the drawing-room ornaments is often undertaken by a member of the family. This frees the housemaid and enables her to get on with other more important duties.

When it becomes dark she must visit each bed-room, draw down the blinds and close the curtains. A can of hot water should be put in readiness in each room. These preparations can be made about an hour and a half before the time of dressing for dinner in a large establishment. Then, when the family are assembled at the meal, the housemaid will return to the bed-rooms, re-arrange the washstand, and set the room in order for the night. Candles should be placed in readiness, the candlesticks having been cleaned during the morning.

An energetic housemaid will get through her work in good time, and have leisure to sew for her mistress if required to do so.

Parlourmaid

A parlourmaid's duties are practically those which would be performed by a single manservant. She is usually kept in those households where no lady's-maid is found, in order that she may perform little services for her mistress.

House-parlourmaid

In small establishments, where few servants are retained, one maid is engaged to perform the joint services of parlourmaid and housemaid.

Between-girl
The between-girl is generally a young maid-servant who spends part of her time in the kitchen assisting the cook, and part in the bed-rooms, etc., helping the housemaid.

Laundrymaid
The services of a laundrymaid are seldom requisitioned, except in large houses in the country. The difficulty of conducting laundry work satisfactorily in a large town is sufficient reason for the work to be sent to the professional laundress.

The laundrymaid generally performs her duties in a separate part of the house, either quite detached from the main building or else only communicating with it by a yard or passage. The building will comprise a wash-house, a room for ironing purposes, with properly constructed stoves, and probably presses or cupboards in which the various articles may be thoroughly dried.

General Servant
The duties of a general servant are numerous. If she is inclined to waste her time, or be unwilling over her work, her duties will become very arduous. In most cases help from outside is occasionally hired by the mistress for particular parts of the work. For example, in turning out rooms and in washing, she will find extra help essential if the wheels of the household are to run smoothly. The hands of the general servant are often already so full that she cannot be responsible for further duties.

Cook-general
Where two or three servants are kept, and the kitchen work is undertaken by one servant only, she is designated a cook-general. Not only is the cooking assigned to her, but various items of housework also. The hall, stairs, and dining-room, or breakfast-room, will doubtless be placed under her care. In small establishments the whole of the housework is often divided between a cook-general and a house-parlourmaid.

Sewing-maid
The sewing-maid is oftenest found in families where there are many young

ladies, and where means are moderate. As the children grow beyond the age at which the services of a nurse are indispensable, the mother finds that some responsible person is necessary to help to keep their wardrobes in good order and repair. Perhaps the family income does not warrant the engagement of a lady's-maid, and a sewing-maid's services are therefore requisitioned.

She should be very skilful in plain sewing, able to cut out and make all kinds of underwear, and have some knowledge of dressmaking. A sewing-maid should be handy and clever in contriving and renovating. By this means she will save her mistress much expense by enabling her to use up garments that might otherwise have to be discarded. By turning and patching, and by skilful adaptation, the best is made of every article of clothing. In a large family of girls the dressmaker's bill can be surprisingly curtailed by the ingenuity of a clever sewing-maid. She should study fashion books and papers, and try to keep her ideas up to date.

Nurse

The head-nurse is responsible for the general arrangement of the nurseries. The youngest child in the nursery will be her special charge. She should, from the very first, endeavour to inculcate good habits in the child.

In her personal appearance and habits the nurse should be invariably neat and clean. Her work is light and never menial, so she will have no excuse for dirty aprons and soiled hands. Of course the nursery routine will, to a certain extent, disarrange her dress, but she should endeavour to make herself tidy again as soon as possible.

The nurse generally takes her meals in the nursery with the children, if she works single-handed, or afterwards if there are nursemaids working under her. The nurse should be clever with her needle, for she will have many hours which can be profitably spent sewing for her mistress or for the small inhabitants of the nursery.

In most cases the nurse's outdoor exercise is assured, for she has to take her little charges for walks, and at the same time her own health benefits by the time spent in the open air. The nurse should not allow constant eating and drinking between meals, and should discourage excessive sweet-eating. In the matter of health, the nurse should never presume to dose the children herself, but act only under the doctor's orders.

The single-handed nursemaid will probably need some assistance with the rougher parts of the nursery work. Either the general servant or the housemaid will help to keep the nurseries clean, scrubbing the floors, laying the fires, and bringing the meals up from the kitchen. The exact organisation of the work should rest with the mistress, and she should do all in her power to let each maid know quite definitely what work she is expected to do. In this way little difficulties which might arise are smoothed over, and each servant can perform her work satisfactorily.

Charwoman
The duties of charwomen vary more widely, perhaps, than those of any other servant. In the generality of cases her work will supplement that of the ordinary domestic servant. Many mistresses arrange for a woman to come in once or twice a week to do the roughest household work, such as beating mats, and all kinds of rough cleaning. She is generally paid by the hour or day, at the rate, in a town, of about 2s. or 2s.6d. a day.